Lighterage tugs

We commence our look at lighterage tugs with the first of a number of views taken on 26 June 1976. The occasion was the Thames Barge Driving Races which coincided with the hottest day of the year in London, when temperatures reached a stifling 34°C. The *Ham* is a Dutch-built tug dating from 1925 and is viewed from Southwark Bridge. She was built by T van Duijvendijk of Lekkerkerk as a steam tug for Robert Neal Tough of Teddington. She passed to Tough & Henderson in 1931 and was motorised in 1961.

From 1966 her owners were Clements Tough Ltd, London. Between 1969 and 1978 she was owned by the Dickinson Robinson Group whose colours she wears in this photograph. In 1978 she began working for Thames & General Lighterage Co Ltd. Changing hands on a number of subsequent occasions, the *Ham* sank in late 1981 but was raised and repaired. Her first change of name came in 1982 when she became the *Nipaway* for J T Palmer & Sons of Gravesend. She was reported broken up in 2004.

(The late C C Beazley)

1

The Royal Observatory at Greenwich has been nicely framed between the towers of the Old Royal Naval College, as the Mercantile Lighterage owned tug **Breezy** passes, heading upstream with her tow. The **Breezy** is an old vessel built in 1914 as a steam tug by Rennie Forrestt at Wivenhoe. She was delivered to James W Cook & Co Ltd, London and remained in their fleet until 1958 when taken over by Cory Lighterage. This is most probably the point at which she was converted to a motor tug, gaining a 390bhp Polar diesel. In 1962 Cory transferred the **Breezy** to their Mercantile Lighterage fleet. This view of her dates from the late summer of 1968, and by the end of the year she had been withdrawn from service. The **Breezy** was scrapped at Grays by T W Ward Ltd in early 1971.

(The late C C Beazley)

The **John White** had been built by J I Thornycroft & Co Ltd at Woolston as the motor tug **Irande** and delivered in 1929 to Thames Steam Tug and Lighterage Co Ltd, London. As such she was fitted with an Ingersoll Rand diesel of 340bhp and boasted a tall folding steam tug-type funnel. In 1947 her original power unit was replaced by a National Gas and Oil Engine diesel. In 1963 the **Irande** was sold to Thames & General Lighterage Ltd who then sold her on to W E White & Sons (Towage) Ltd, London, in 1970.

She became the **John White** in 1973 under the ownership of Thomas J Dilks later passing to Alfred E White, London. This is how we see her in the Upper Pool on a rather misty 30 April 1978. Thames & Medway Towage Co Ltd (Ron Livett), Rochester, were her new owners from 1983. Her name was changed back to **Irande** in 1985. She is believed to have been was scrapped in 1992 at Rainham, Kent.

(Nigel Jones)

In 1894 the impressive Tower Bridge was opened making it the final bridge crossing of the Thames downstream. The Corporation of London required a tug to be present on standby duties at Tower Bridge to assist any ships having difficulty passing between the two towers. Gaselee provided a tug for this duty for many years. J P Knight Ltd based at Rochester were principally engaged in ship-handling and lighterage operation on the River Medway, but also worked on the River Thames. The *Kawara* dated from 1934 and had been built by James Pollock Sons & Co at Faversham for J P Knight. She had a 455bhp British Polar diesel engine and is seen on duty at Tower Bridge in November 1971. This was the period following the amalgamation of Gaselee & Son Ltd with J P Knight Ltd on 30 August 1966, to form Gaselee & Knight Ltd. The *Kawara* lasted in service until 1973, whereupon she was despatched to Thomas W Ward Ltd for breaking up at Grays.

(Bernard McCall collection)

This rather atmospheric shot of the small lighterage tug *Impermo* was taken in July 1972. A vessel of just 38 tons gross she began life as the *Temeritie*, and was delivered to Medway Oil & Storage Co Ltd, Rochester, in 1937 from the yard of Richard Dunston Ltd, Thorne. She was twin-screw and was powered by a pair of Crossley diesels with a combined output of 200bhp. She was sold to Shell-Mex & BP Ltd, London, in 1953 and had several further owners eventually taking the unofficial name *Benbow* for Samuel Williams & Sons Ltd, London, in 1956. She became the *Impermo* in 1959 after passing to The Associated Portland Cement Manufacturers Ltd. Here she was managed by Blue Circle Shipping Ltd, London, who later became her owners in 1970. She was last heard of in the same year as this photo when she was sold to T G Hooper at Wrotham.

(The late C C Beazley)

On 26 June 1976 the **Caroline Bodkin** was working for Erith & Dartford Lighterage Co Ltd, Erith, and is seen from Southwark Bridge, looking a little shabby. She had carried three previous names and was built in 1937 by Henry Scarr of Hessle as the **Isleworth Lion** for Lion Wharf Ltd, London. In 1959 she was sold to General Lighterage Co Ltd and her Widdop engine was replaced with a 4-cyl Crossley. She became **General V** in 1960 and passed to Erith & Dartford Lighterage in 1962, becoming **Caroline Bodkin** in 1975. In 1983 her owners changed their title to Dartford Warehousing & Transport Ltd, Erith, and the **Caroline Bodkin** was sold the following year. In 1989 she passed to Medway Towing Services who renamed her **Caroline**, and by 2004 she was in Hoo Marina in use as a houseboat.

(The late C C Beazley)

With Greenwich Power Station as a backdrop, the 1937-built **Robertsbridge** is seen making her way up the Thames in July 1971. She was completed by J I Thornycroft & Co Ltd, Woolston, as a diesel-electric tug of 530bhp for Thames Steam Tug & Lighterage Co Ltd of London. The **Robertsbridge** had a gross tonnage of 90 and was powered by a pair of Ruston diesels driving a pair of BTH generators and motors geared to a single propeller. In 1962 her machinery was replaced by a 450bhp diesel and conventional transmission. Her owner was restyled Thames & General Lighterage Co Ltd in 1963 following a merger with the General Lighterage Co, and in 1975 she was renamed **General VI**. She passed to Mercantile Lighterage Ltd in 1980 and went on charter to Underwater Services in 1981 as **Barra Reef**. The deal fell through and the tug passed to Cory Lighterage Ltd, and she was renamed **General VI**. She was last heard of in 1982 when she passed to Mayhew of Queenborough.

(The late C C Beazley)

Launch tugs which were often known as Toshers were small tugs that featured internal combustion engines and were designed to work within dock systems, canals and creeks. They were shallow draught vessels with little or no accommodation and could usually pass under closed swing bridges. This view of the **Duckett** was taken from Blackfriars Bridge during the Thames Barge Driving Races in 1976. It gives the reader a superb view of her uncluttered deck, emphasising the lack of bulwarks. She was built in 1938 by J Pollock Sons & Co Ltd of Faversham for service with Thames Steam Tug & Lighterage Co, London, and was powered by a diesel of 180bhp. In 1972 the **Duckett** passed to E M Mayhew and later W E White & Sons. By 1992 she was with Tilbury Douglas Construction, Erith, and in 2006 was still in service for Spithead Trading Ltd, Braintree.

(The late C C Beazley)

On 16 July 1976 the Cory tug *Hurricane* is photographed approaching Westminster Bridge with several well-laden barges in tow. An attractive tug, she has a prominent raked bow and a distinctive wheelhouse. The *Hurricane* dates from 1938 and was built for James W Cook & Co Ltd, London, by Henry Scarr Ltd of Hessle on Humberside. In 1958 Cook was taken over by Cory and she passed to Mercantile Lighterage Co Ltd.

The *Hurricane* was later rebuilt gaining the enclosed wheelhouse seen here. In 1983 she was sold to Braithwaite & Dean Lighterage Ltd, London, who kept her until about 1994. The *Hurricane* was then laid up falling into a state of dereliction at Deptford Creek, later being towed away to Leigh-on-Sea and being put up for sale. It is thought she was scrapped in about 2007.

(The late C C Beazley)

The Dutch-built *Wal* of 1938 was one of four similar vessels completed by T van Duijvendijk, Lekkerkerk. She was delivered to W R Cunis Ltd of Woolwich and was just 14 tons gross. She had a 2-cyl Bolinder diesel and between 15 July 1942 and 17 December 1945 was requisitioned by the Ministry of War Transport at a hire rate of £29 6s 8d per day. After the war the *Wal* continued in service for Cunis, passing to Gaselee & Knight Ltd in 1967. When this arrangement ceased she was retained by J P Knight, subsequently passing through a number of owners in Essex from 1980. She then passed to Riley Banks Marine Ltd in 1985 taking the new name *Beaver II*. A further string of owners followed from 1986 during which time she sank. By 1994 she had been repaired and put back in service and was last heard of in 1999 in the Medway area. We see her in J P Knight ownership, just off Gravesend, in October 1971.

(The late C C Beazley)

The **Vassal** was an example of a Jubilee class launch tug from the shipyard of James Pollock & Co Ltd at Faversham. Pollock built twelve of these between 1935 and 1950, and the **Vassal** was completed in 1938. From new she worked for Vokins & Co Ltd, London, until they sold her in 1975 to Thames & General Lighterage Ltd. She passed to Cory Lighterage in 1980 and General Marine Ltd in 1982 who altered her name to **Vassel** for some reason. She was eventually destined to leave the Thames in 2008 passing to an owner in Yorkshire who removed her engine and propeller shaft, and was then put up for sale at Hull. In 2014 she was purchased for restoration as Vokin's **Vassal**, and moved to the Waldringfield boatyard on the River Deben in Suffolk. Also in this view and alongside the **Vassal** we see the launch tug **Express**. We do not know where or when she was built but she was originally owned by General Lighterage Ltd, London, and from 1963 was with Thames & General Lighterage Ltd. She was with Cory Lighterage Co Ltd from 1980, and after numerous subsequent owners was to be found in 2005 lying at Pipers Wharf, Greenwich, in a sorry state. The **Express** was then refurbished in 2008 and fitted with a new Volvo diesel engine in 2010 and was back at work soon after.

(The late C C Beazley)

With her distinctive red superstructure and white funnel, the **Arthur Darling** would have been easy to spot from a distance. She was completed in 1946 as **John Hawkins** for John Hawkins Ltd, London. She was built in Essex by Rowhedge Ironworks Co of Rowhedge and had a gross tonnage of 50. She was powered by a British Polar diesel of 295bhp, which gave her a speed of 10 knots. In 1970 **John Hawkins** was sold to M Tugs Ltd, London, passing later that year to Darling Bros Ltd, London, who renamed the tug **Arthur Darling**. This photo shows the **Arthur Darling** heading up the Thames and passing the splendid Trafalgar Tavern public house at Greenwich, which dates from around 1837. The tug was sold by Darling Bros Ltd in 1977 and is believed to have been exported to the Middle East by 1979.

(The late C C Beazley)

From the very early days all lighterage tugs featured fold-down masts to enable them to pass under bridges, while steam powered examples also had fold-down funnels. In 1943 Richard Dunston Ltd of Thorne completed the small lighterage tug **Pinklake** for the River Lighterage Co Ltd, London. She was a steam powered tug that featured a triple expansion engine of 400ihp and had a gross tonnage of 87. She was sold to W E White & Sons (Towage) Ltd, London in 1960 passing to F T Everard & Sons Lighterage Ltd of Greenhithe the following year. They changed her name to **R. A. Everard** and rebuilt her into a motor tug during 1962 using a secondhand Newbury diesel, losing her tall funnel in the process. Here we see her in action on the Thames in about 1975, passing HMS **President** and heading towards Blackfriars Bridge. In 1990 she became the **Carole A.** for H C H Services Ltd, Greenhithe who kept her until 2010, whereupon she was sold for use as a houseboat at Faversham.

(The late C C Beazley)

The **Vortex** was a motor tug built in 1947 as **Snowcem** for owners The Associated Portland Cement Manufacturers (1900) Ltd, London. She was completed by Henry Scarr Ltd, Hessle, and was powered by a 6-cyl British Polar diesel of 465bhp. In 1962 she passed to Vokins & Co Ltd as **Vortex** and this is how we see her on 2 July 1973, passing Island Gardens opposite Greenwich with the small swim lighter **Ditchley** lashed to her starboard side. Two years later she was working for Thames and General Lighterage Co Ltd as **General III** passing to Cory Lighterage Ltd, London, in 1980. At some point in the 1980s she was sold by Cory to General Marine Services, London, and by 2003 had been converted to a houseboat at Hoo, Kent. In 2010 she was still noted as such, but had relocated to Deptford Creek just off the Thames near Greenwich.

(The late C C Beazley)

The *Hawkstone* was completed for Mercantile Lighterage Co Ltd, London, in 1948 at the yard of Richard Dunston Ltd, Thorne. She was fitted with a two-stroke British Polar diesel of 450bhp which gave her a speed of 9½ knots. The *Hawkstone* was later transferred to Cory Tank Lighterage Ltd, London. On 25 February 1958 she departed Canvey Island with the tank barges *Stonecourt* and *Stonemoor* in tow. The barges were destined for the River Medway, and it was the intention to hand these over to the tug *Crowstone* at some point. The *Hawkstone* would then proceed to the Thames. The weather was poor and the *Hawkstone* appears to have taken on water before becoming overwhelmed by the sea. The crew of six were lost and the tug was later found abandoned on a sandbank in the Thames estuary. The *Hawkstone* was recovered, repaired and put back into service. Here we see her leaving the Royal Docks in July 1970. In 1980 she was broken up at Blackwall.

(The late C C Beazley)

The *Revenge* was another lighterage tug that began life in the Cory fleet on the Thames. In this early morning photograph taken in October 1996, she is seen in the heart of London just below London Bridge, having not long joined the fleet of General Marine Ltd. She was completed in 1948 by Richard Dunston Ltd, Thorne, as *Revenge* for Cory Lighterage Ltd. She had a gross tonnage of 61 and was fitted with a 330bhp Crossley diesel, which was later replaced by a more powerful diesel. In 1982 she was sold to Lee & Brentford Lighterage, and in 1996 to General Marine Ltd, London, who were still operating her in 2016.

(Bernard McCall)

The *Velox* is another launch tug that it is thought still survives. She has an overall length of 41 feet and was built in 1949 by Richard Dunston Ltd at Thorne. She was powered by a 120bhp diesel engine and was delivered to Clements, Knowling & Co Ltd, London. However by 1950 she had passed to the Port of London Authority and in this view is seen moored at one of PLA's landing stages. The *Velox* remained with the PLA until moving to the fleet of London River Services at some point after 1998. Her subsequent movements seem a little unclear but it is believed that she was with Crouch River Services, Burnham-on-Crouch, from about 2007, and later had a bow thruster unit fitted. In 2013 she passed to S Holly at Rochford for use in conjunction with dredging projects in the Essex area.

(Andrew Wiltshire collection)

The **Mercedes II** was built in 1949 as **Silverbeam** and was delivered new to Silvertown Services Lighterage Ltd, London. She was another product of James Pollock's yard at Faversham and had a gross tonnage of 92. In 1971 she passed to Mercantile Lighterage Ltd as **Mercedes II** and was repainted into William Cory's distinctive black and white livery. From new she had a 615bhp British Polar diesel, but this was replaced in 1972 by a more powerful 800bhp Lister Blackstone unit. She was sold in 1982 passing to Darling Bros Ltd and then to Cleanaway Ltd as **Jean Raby** (see below).

(Bernard McCall collection)

The movement of London's refuse in barges along the River Thames has been an important function for several decades and tugs can be seen passing right through the heart of London with a procession of barges in tow. Originally their destination would have been the land reclamation sites on the Essex Marshes. Cleanaway Ltd were based at Rainham and deployed a small fleet of elderly tugs for towing refuse barges. These included the **William Ryan** of 1908, the **Jim Higgs** of 1959 and the **Jean Raby** of 1949 (see above). With empty refuse barges in tow, the **Jean Raby** is seen approaching Lambeth Bridge on 9 June 1986. In 2003 the **Jean Raby** regained her earlier name **Silverbeam** when she was sold to Medway Towing Services Ltd. She was still at work in 2016.

(Andrew Wiltshire)

This view at the Thames Barge Driving Races on 26 June 1976 features the classic lighterage tug **Sandtex** which is in immaculate condition for the event. She is a vessel of 92 tons gross, and was yet another small tug completed by James Pollock Sons & Co Ltd of Faversham. She was delivered to Silvertown Services Lighterage Ltd in July 1950 as **Silverdial**, and passed to Associated Portland Cement Manufacturing Co in 1970. She was renamed **Sandtex** and was managed by Blue Circle Shipping. She was initially sold in 1983 to AAP Tugs, Rainham, Kent, and by 1988 had moved north to owners at Hartlepool who converted her to a diving support vessel. She received a substantial new superstructure which made her unrecognisable as a former lighterage tug. However this was later removed, and by 2012 she was lying in Tees Dock in a derelict state.

(The late C C Beazley)

In 1951 the Port of London Authority received three small launch tugs from the yard of James Pollock Sons & Co Ltd. The first was the **Placate** with yard number 1940 followed by the slightly smaller **Plashy** and **Plaudit** which were yard numbers 1941 and 1942. Now in her 25th year, the **Placate** is viewed from Southwark Bridge having attended the 1976 Barge Driving Races. She has a gross tonnage of 24 and her propulsion is by a 152bhp Crossley diesel driving a single screw. Some uncertainty surrounds her whereabouts after she was sold by the PLA in the late 1970s. However it is thought that in 2016 the **Placate** is to be found in the Canvey Island area of Essex. She has been modified with the addition of a cabin, and is in use as a static houseboat, a role she has probably been fulfilling for a good number of years.

(The late C C Beazley)

The **Recruit** was a sister ship to the **Swiftstone** also of 1952, and was completed by Richard Dunston Ltd, Thorne, for Cory Tank Lighterage Ltd, London. She had a gross tonnage of 91, an overall length of 80 feet and her main power came from a 670bhp Crossley diesel engine. In 1983 she was transferred into the Cory Waste Management Ltd fleet, passing in 1990 to Cory Environmental Ltd. The **Recruit** went on to receive a Mirrlees Blackstone engine in 1996 which gave her an enhanced bollard pull of 11 tonnes. At this point the opportunity was taken to modernise the tug and she gained a new wheelhouse, a pusher knee to her bow, and was fitted with low-profile twin funnels. This is how we see the **Recruit** in May 2003.

(Barry Crickmore)

Having been replaced by newer tugs, the **Recruit** was sold to Thameside Services Ltd, Gravesend in 2011. She then passed to GPS Marine Ltd of Chatham, and was given a thorough refit and renamed **GPS Cervia**, before joining their River and Light Towage fleet. On 10 April 2015 the **GPS Cervia** makes her way upstream with a laden aggregates barge alongside. In this view taken from on board HMS **Belfast** she is passing the Tower of London, and heading for a construction site in the Battersea area.

(Andrew Wiltshire)

The **Showery** was the final vessel in a quartet of launch tugs delivered between 1948 and 1952 from the yard of James W Cook (Wivenhoe) Ltd, Wivenhoe. She followed her sisters **Cloudy** (1948), **Hazy** (1949) and **Misty** (1951), all being delivered to James W Cook & Co Ltd, London, for use on the Thames. The Thames-based lighterage interests of James W Cook were taken over in 1958 by Cory Lighterage Ltd and in 1961, the **Showery** was placed in their Mercantile Lighterage subsidiary fleet. In her Mercantile Lighterage days she is seen heading downstream past Island Gardens on an overcast 14 July 1976. She was sold in 1983 to J Read and then on to Hastings Brothers Ltd of Brentwood in 1987. She was last heard of in 2009 sailing as **Pablo** for Max Couper of Battersea.

(The late C C Beazley)

This superb view of the **Blackboys** was taken in October 1968. She is on the river near Greenwich. The **Blackboys** was built at the Brentford-based yard of E C Jones & Son (Brentford) Ltd in 1958 and delivered to Thames Steam Tug & Lighterage Co Ltd, London. She had a gross tonnage of 22 and an overall length of 46 feet. The **Blackboys** passed to Thames and General Lighterage Co Ltd in 1963 and eventually received the new name **General V** in 1970. Further changes of ownership saw her with Cory Lighterage Co Ltd from 1980, and J Darling from 1982. She continued to work on the Thames and was renamed **Caspar C** in 1984 for her next owner Cleanaway Ltd, London. By this point she had gained a rather crude wheelhouse. Despite her age she passed to the Environment Agency, London, in 2002 and was renamed **Falconbrook**. By 2006 she sported a modern-looking wheelhouse, and was still in service in 2014.

(The late C C Beazley)

The **St. Olaf** is very smartly turned out for the occasion of the Thames Barge Driving Races. She was built in North Devon by P K Harris & Sons Ltd of Appledore and delivered in 1956 to B Jacob & Sons Ltd, London. She had a gross tonnage of 37 and was powered by a 360bhp diesel. In this view the **St. Olaf** is working for Humphrey & Grey (Lighterage) Ltd and in 1980 passed to McCann Tugs Ltd, London as **G. P. McCann**. She left the Thames area in 1986 to work in Fleetwood as **St. Olaf** once more, before returning to the Thames again in 1999. By 2006 she had been converted to a houseboat and was last noted at Barking Creek in 2011.

(The late C C Beazley)

The **Niparound** is seen approaching the landing stage at Gravesend on 8 May 1970. This tug started out in 1957 as **Beckton II**. She was completed by Richard Dunston Ltd at Thorne for service with the North Thames Gas Board. She had an overall length of 62 feet, a gross tonnage of 43 and was powered by a 202bhp diesel engine. In this view she is operating for J T Palmer & Sons of Gravesend, into whose fleet she had passed in 1965, gaining the name **Niparound**. She eventually left the Thames in the late 1970s for a new life in Scotland with J Dinwoodie & Sons of Granton. She sank at Inverary in October 1982 but was raised and returned to service. By 1987 she had been re-engined and rebuilt. In 2002 she was noted lying derelict on a Shetland beach.

(The late John Wiltshire)

This undated view shows the tug *Regard* passing the Trafalgar Tavern at Greenwich, with the barge *Mercator* in tow. The *Mercator* was a special catamaran barge built by Cory at their barge works in early 1970 for The Mercantile Lighterage Co Ltd. It was used to transport Ford cars upriver from the Dagenham car plant in Essex. Here it is carrying just over 50 Mk2 Ford Cortinas. The tug *Regard* was built in 1958 by James W Cook (Wivenhoe) Ltd and delivered to Cory Lighterage Ltd, London. Her main engine was a Ruston & Hornsby diesel of 409bhp which was replaced in 1974 with a slightly more powerful Lister Blackstone unit. She remained with Cory until 1982 when she passed to Erith & Dartford Lighterage Co Ltd. She was renamed *Sir James D.*, being resold to Braithwaite & Dean in 1984, who changed her name back to *Regard*. In 1991 she became the *Regarder* for Alan C Bennett & Sons Ltd and was eventually scrapped in 2014 at Greenhithe. It is thought that the barge *Mercator* later formed the basis of a houseboat on the Thames.

(The late C C Beazley)

The three tugs *Lord Devonport*, *Lord Ritchie* and *Lord Waverley* were built by James Pollock Sons & Co at Faversham for the Port of London Authority (PLA) and were allocated to the dredging fleet. The *Lord Devonport* was delivered in 1959, while the other two followed in 1960. In this view we see the *Lord Waverley* with a barge passing Island Gardens in September 1971. The *Lord Ritchie* was sold in 1977, but the surviving pair continued in use with the PLA for many more years, passing to Port of Tilbury Ltd in 1992. In 1993 the *Lord Waverley* was sold to Nigerian interests in a deal that was not concluded, and it is thought that she then passed to General Marine Services Ltd, London, in 2005 for resale along with *Lord Devonport*.

(The late C C Beazley)

The *Lord Devonport* and *Lord Waverley* each had a gross tonnage of 109 and an overall length of 84 feet. They were powered by a 5-cyl British Polar diesel of 935bhp and had a bollard pull of 18 tonnes. The *Lord Devonport* is seen here as recently as July 2009, and is believed to be in the ownership of General Marine Ltd, London. On this occasion both tugs were out on the river and on test, maybe for a potential buyer. Along with the *Lord Waverley,* the pair had spent a considerable amount of time laid up and for sale since 1993. The *Lord Devonport* and *Lord Waverley* later moved to Richborough in Kent by April 2011, and in 2016 were noted moored at Ramsgate, both in poor condition.

(Barry Crickmore)

In September 1975 the *General VII* is seen heading downstream past Lovell's Wharf at Greenwich. She is another vessel of Thames & General Lighterage Ltd and was completed in 1962 for the General Lighterage Co Ltd, London. She was a tug of 64grt with an overall length of 75 feet and completed at Thorne by Richard Dunston. With the amalgamation of her owner with Thames Steam Tug & Lighterage Co Ltd in 1963, she became part of the new Thames & General Lighterage Ltd with whom she continued to sail until 1980. The business then passed to Cory Lighterage Co Ltd, London, at this point in time. On 16 October 1985 the *General VII* was in collision with the British flag bulk carrier *Rora Head* (of 1980) in the Thames estuary. Four out of her crew of seven were tragically lost. The tug was soon raised and broken up.

(The late C C Beazley)

The **Sir Aubrey** started out as a member of Humphrey & Grey (Lighterage) Ltd fleet in 1962. With a gross tonnage of 59 she was built by Richard Dunston Ltd at Thorne and was powered by a 457bhp diesel. In 1977 she was re-engined with a more powerful Lister Blackstone unit and eventually passed to London & Rochester Trading Co Ltd, Strood, in 1983. In 1984 she became **Margaret Barry** for Thames Marine & Civil Engineering Ltd, but reverted to **Sir Aubrey** in 1988 when acquired by Carolcraft Ltd, London. It is in that fleet that we see her at work at Tilbury on 5 June 2004. The **Sir Aubrey** then passed to General Marine Services, London, in 2005 and saw some service but was laid up by 2009 in a generally poor condition. Renovation began but was never finished. By 2014 she was engineless and advertised for sale for use as a houseboat.

(Ian Willett)

The **Lingo** was a late example of a traditional Thames lighterage tug being completed in 1964. The tug follows fairly traditional lines but lacks a funnel having a crude exhaust pipe in its place. She was one of the relatively few tugs built in Dorset at the yard of J Bolson & Sons Ltd, Poole, and was last newbuilding for her owner Union Lighterage Co Ltd. This view of **Lingo** taken in July 1970 portrays the tug passing Highbridge Wharf near Greenwich. In 1971 she was sold to Lambert Barge Hire Ltd and was later chartered to Cory Lighterage Ltd. Her next change of owner was to Mercantile Lighterage Co Ltd, who renamed her **Merit**. By 1990 she was operating on the Thames for Cory Enviromental Ltd and engaged in towing refuse barges. In 1993 her engine was replaced by a more powerful Mirrlees Blackstone unit, and around this time she gained two funnels and her wheelhouse was rebuilt. The **Merit** had been sold by Cory by 2012, and was being refitted for a new owner in 2016.

(The late C C Beazley)

The lighterage tug was once numerous on the Thames, but by the late 1960s their numbers were rapidly diminishing as the enclosed docks and river wharves were closed down. The *Friston Down* is captured passing the Old Royal Naval College at Greenwich in October 1968. The tug was completed by Richard Dunston Ltd at Thorne and delivered to Humphrey & Grey (Lighterage) Ltd, London, in October 1964. The *Friston Down* had a gross tonnage of 99 and was originally powered by a British Polar 2-stroke diesel of 560bhp. In 1983 she was sold to London & Rochester Trading Co Ltd (Crescent Shipping), Rochester, and by 1993 had been purchased by General Port Services Ltd, London. Her original engine was replaced in 1996 by a Caterpillar diesel which gave her a bollard pull of 21 tonnes. The tug received machinery damage in July 2012 when her propeller became fouled, but she was repaired and returned to service. By 2013 the title of her owner had changed to GPS Marine Contractors Ltd, Chatham, and the *Friston Down* was sporting the new name *GPS Anglia*.

(The late C C Beazley)

The Port of London Authority's unusual pusher tug **Broodbank** is seen underway off Tilbury on 18 July 1991. She is in charge of the PLA grab barge **Albert** both vessels being part of the dredging division. The **Broodbank** was completed in 1966 by James W Cook (Wivenhoe) Ltd of Wivenhoe for the PLA. She was a very manoeuvrable vessel of 189 gross tons and was fitted with a pair of Schottel SRP 225 propulsion units. These were driven by two Rolls-Royce turbocharged diesel engines developing a total of 1000bhp. Her overall length as built was just 56 feet but she had a substantial breadth of 31 feet. She remained with her owner for 28 years spending much of this time active in the dredging unit. She passed to Briggs Marine Contractors Ltd of Burntisland in 1994, and was rebuilt into a workboat. She had a 37 foot forward section of hull added as well as a new wheelhouse. This work was completed in 1995 and she emerged as the **Forth Constructor**. She is believed to be still in action in 2017, but with new engines and propulsion units.

(Stuart Emery)

In 1979 Cory was awarded a major contract by the Greater London Council to transport London's refuse downstream by barge. At this point a fleet of around eight former lighterage tugs was employed and managed by Cory Waste Management, Domestic Division. The newest tug at this time was the **General VIII** which was completed in 1965 for Thames and General Lighterage Co. Ltd, London, by Richard Dunston's Thorne yard. When her owner was taken over in 1980 by William Cory & Son (Cory Lighterage Ltd), she was part of the deal. The **General VIII** gained a replacement engine in 1990 in the form of an 1196bhp Lister Blackstone diesel. This view of her dates from 10 April 1997 and clearly shows her modernised wheelhouse. During the 1990s the new title of her owner was Cory Environmental Ltd - Pollution Control Services, and in 2011 she was sold to an owner at Brentford. By 2012 the **General VIII** was back in the Cory fleet, but by 2013 had passed to General Marine Services Ltd, London.

(Bernard McCall)

The **Horton** is a small motor tug of 31grt that was built in 1968 for the Blyth Harbour Commissioners. She was completed by Richard Dunston Ltd, Thorne, as a replacement for the much larger twin-screw steam tug **Chipchase**. The **Horton** had an 8-cyl Bergius-Kelvin diesel of 243bhp and a speed of 8 knots. After just five years she was sold to The Fleetwood Fishing Vessel Owners Association Ltd, Fleetwood, passing on to M Tugs Ltd, London, in 1979 as **D. A. McCann**. In 1986 she began working for A W Marine Ltd, Westcliff, and was renamed **Horton** once again. In 1997 she was re-engined, and eventually sold in May 2009 to J T Palmer & Sons Ltd who are based at Gravesend. She continues to work for J T Palmer in this photograph taken at Northfleet on 24 February 2016.

(Ian Willett)

The modern-looking single-screw tug *Evelyn Spearing II* was still a relatively new vessel in this view from Southwark Bridge during the Thames Barge Driving Races. Little is known about her except that she was built in 1976 at Greenhithe by W G S Crouch & Sons Ltd for use in their own fleet. Her owner's larger than life house flag flies above her wheelhouse. She was sold in 1986 to L Tester and subsequently chartered to Thameside Services Ltd. She was later with Charman Towage who shortened her name to *Evelyn Spearing*. Her fate is unknown and was last heard of advertised for sale in 2003.

(The late C C Beazley)

The *Lashette* and the *Grey Lash* were a pair of similar pusher tugs completed by London & Rochester Trading Co Ltd at Strood for use handling barges discharged by LASH (Lighter Aboard Ship) vessels. The *Lashette* was delivered in 1971 for its own account, while the *Grey Lash* was delivered in 1974 to Humphrey & Grey (Lighterage) Ltd, London. They both featured a pair of Schottel propulsion units. The *Grey Lash* is seen on 14 July 1976 passing the Trafalgar Tavern at Greenwich towing a lighter over her stern. In 1983 she passed to London & Rochester Trading Co Ltd (Crescent Shipping Ltd), Rochester, and became the *Shovette*. She changed hands in 1998 when sold to Deutsche Binnenreederei (UK) Ltd, London, and again in 2001 when she left the Thames area and moved to Humberside for a future with Deans Tugs & Workboats Ltd (John Dean) at Hull.

(The late C C Beazley)

This fascinating scene at Tilbury on 29 June 2002 shows Palmer's tug **Unico** about to tow a barge out of the bows of barge/container carrying vessel **Baco-Liner 2**. The **Unico** was built in 1927 by J S Watson (Gainsborough) Ltd at Gainsborough for service with Union Lighterage Co Ltd, London. She was just 51grt and was powered by a 200bhp Gardner engine. In 1971 she passed to J T Palmer & Sons, Gravesend, and was finally broken up in July 2013 at Gravesend, having never changed her name. The **Baco-Liner 2** (new in 1980) was one of a series of three similar ships specially built to carry barges and containers between northern Europe and ports in West Africa. The ships were built for Seerederei Bacoliner GmbH of Hamburg by Thyssen Nordseewerke GmbH of Emden and placed under the Liberian flag. They could carry 12 barges and up to 650TEU size containers. The service appears to have ended by 2010 and all three ships were scrapped. The **Baco-Liner 2** met her end at Gadani Beach in 2013.

(Ian Willett)

From 1985 London's refuse was containerised and shipped in 20 new purpose-built barges. The first new purpose-built tug for the Cory Environmental PLC fleet on the Thames was the twin-screw *Regain*. She was completed in the Netherlands at Sliedrecht by Delta Shipyard and delivered to her owners in December 1997. She has rather distinctive lines with quite a high bow and a gross tonnage of 138. Her engines are a pair of 8-cyl Caterpillar diesels with a combined output of 1610bhp that give her a bollard pull of 17½ tonnes. This view of the *Regain* was taken at Tilbury on 29 May 2009. She is working hard judging by the heat haze from her exhaust.

(Simon Smith)

This second view of the *Regain* was taken on 16 June 2016 from London Bridge. It gives the reader a completely different perspective of the tug's overall design, and a clear view of her towing gear in action. She is quite unlike any other tug to have worked on the Thames with her forward accommodation, large wheelhouse and raked funnels. The *Regain* has an overall length of 87 feet, a beam of 30 feet and a draught of 7 feet 6 inches. In 2017 the *Regain* was still in the Cory Environmental fleet, but kept as the spare tug.

(Stuart Emery)

In 2002 Cory Environmental was awarded a 30-year contract to carry municipal waste from the London boroughs of Lambeth, Fulham, Hammersmith and Wandsworth plus the Royal Borough of Kensington and Chelsea. This employed around 47 barges and of course continued to require a fleet of tugs. For delivery in the summer of 2010 to replace much older vessels, Cory ordered four new tugs for its fleet. They were based on the Damen Shoalbuster 2208S design and were given the names *Reclaim, Recovery*, *Redoubt* and *Resource*. This photograph depicts all four tugs on parade in the Upper Pool whilst taking part in the Queen's Diamond Jubilee Pageant on 3 June 2012.

(Stuart Emery)

The new tugs are smaller than the **Regain** (page 30), but are more manoeuvrable featuring a 100bhp bow thruster unit and are designed to work in shallow waters. Based at Cory Environmental's Charlton lighterage base and barge works, they are engaged towing barges from Cory's four upriver wharves, downstream to the Riverside Resource Recovery Facility at Belvedere. This is a large processing plant that was opened in 2011. The incinerator ash from this plant is processed and much of it used in the construction industry. The **Reclaim** is seen here at Woolwich on 12 March 2014. Her own̶e̶r̶s̶ ̶a̶r̶e̶ ̶given as Riverside ̶̶̶̶n̶d̶o̶n̶ ̶and managed by

(Laurie Rufus)

This second view of **Reclaim** was taken just downstream from Tower Bridge on 15 June 2016. It gives us a clear view of her funnel offset to starboard, her towing gear and her large uncluttered aft deck. The heavy stern fendering is essential when handling barges out in the tideway on the river. The **Reclaim** has an overall length of 74 feet with a moulded breadth of 26 feet 3 inches and a loaded draught of just over 6 feet. She is powered by two Vee 12-cyl Caterpillar diesels with a combined output of 1200bhp running at 1800rpm. These drive Promarin fixed-pitch propellers in van der Giessen Optima nozzles, resulting in a bollard pull of 17 tonnes and a free running speed of 10.9 knots.

(Stuart Emery)

Ship-handling tugs

In the 1960s the ship-handling tug played a major role on the Thames. A fleet was still required to serve the upriver enclosed dock systems as well as Tilbury further downstream, together with the oil terminals in the Thames estuary. The **Sun X** was delivered to her owners W H J Alexander Ltd in January 1920 and had a gross tonnage of 196. Her builder was Cochrane & Sons Ltd at Selby, who also completed the similar **Sun VIII** and **Sun IX**. Her machinery consisted of a 700ihp triple expansion engine supplied by steam from a coal-fired boiler. On 18 December 1936 the **Sun X** was sunk after a collision with the Belgian coaster **Turquoise** of 1933, which was outbound from Tilbury docks. The tug was raised the next day and after repair was back in service the following month. In this view the **Sun X** is noted off the King George V entrance lock in 1968 at the end of her working life. She passed to London Tugs Ltd on 27 January 1969, and was towed away to Antwerp for scrapping shortly after.

(The late C C Beazley)

Between 1909 and 1925 Earle's Shipbuilding & Engineering Co Ltd of Hull completed seven tugs for W H J Alexander Ltd (known locally as Sun Tugs). The **Sun XII** was the penultimate example and was delivered in July 1925. She was a steam tug with an overall length of 106 feet and was in most aspects very similar to the **Sun XI** and **Sun XV**. In 1957 the **Sun XII** was converted to oil firing by J S Doig Ltd, Grimsby, and consequently received a new funnel and luffing lifeboat davits. On 27 January 1969 the towage concerns of W H J Alexander and Ship Towage (London) Ltd were amalgamated to form London Tugs Ltd, in a deal that included 36 tugs. This view of the **Sun XII** was taken in early 1969 when her funnel markings had been modified to those of London Tugs Ltd. This era was to prove short-lived, as in May 1969 the tug was sold and towed away to Antwerp to be broken up by Scrappingco SA.

(The late C C Beazley)

The **Dilwara** of 1930 and the very similar **Dongara** of 1932 were the last tugs delivered to Gravesend United Steam Tug Co. They were both completed by Cochrane & Sons Ltd, Selby, to an overall length of 100 feet and were powered by an 825ihp triple expansion steam engine. The **Dilwara** was delivered in September 1930 and renamed **Dendera** in 1935 so that her name was free for use on a new passenger vessel. In June 1937 Gravesend United Steam Tug Co was taken over by William Watkins Ltd, and in June 1938 the **Dendera** was renamed **Racia** and repainted into Watkins house colours. On 1 February 1950 she was incorporated into the Ship Towage (London) Ltd operation and remained in Watkins colours. This view of the **Racia** was taken prior to her receiving Ship Towage colours in 1965. When she was withdrawn the **Racia** was the last large coal-burning tug handling ships on the Thames. She was towed by the **Moorcock** to Boom near Antwerp for breaking up in August 1967.

(Stuart Emery collection)

The **Challenge** was the last operational steam tug on the River Thames when she was eventually taken out of service and sold to Taylor Woodrow for preservation in October 1973. She was moored in St. Katherines Dock London for 19 years, and could well have been scrapped if she had not been rescued by the Dunkirk Little Ships Restoration Trust in 1993. She was moved to Tilbury for restoration and her boiler was fired for the first time in late 1994. The **Challenge** then moved under her own power in 1995. Her restoration as an operational vessel was completed and she went on to receive a new and more efficient boiler in 2013. The **Challenge** was built in 1931 by Alexander Hall & Co Ltd, Aberdeen, and delivered to Elliott Steam Tug Company Ltd of London. She is an important survivor as she was involved in Operation Dynamo, the evacuation from Dunkirk in May/June 1940. She also rescued three survivors from the steam tug **Cervia** which capsized and sank on 25 October 1954. In 1969 she passed to London Tugs Ltd which is how we see her off Gravesend in 1971.

(The late C C Beazley)

The **Atlantic Cock** and her virtually identical sister ship **Ocean Cock** were completed in 1932 and delivered to Gamecock Steam Towing Co Ltd, London, in March that year. They were constructed in Scotland by Alexander Hall & Co Ltd at Aberdeen and had a gross tonnage of 182. The pair were 96 feet in length and were powered by a 900ihp triple expansion steam engine assembled by the shipyard. The subject of our image is the **Atlantic Cock** seen here making some impressive smoke in January 1965. In 1940 she was requisitioned for war service, returning to the Thames in late 1944. On 1 February 1950 she was incorporated into the Ship Towage (London) Ltd operation and remained in Gamecock Steam Towing colours, her ownership eventually transferring to William Watkins Ltd. During 1965 she gained Ship Towage colours and on 27 January 1969 she was absorbed into the newly-formed London Tugs Ltd. Now at the end of her career the **Atlantic Cock** was sold in February 1970 to Scrappingco NV for breaking up at Willebroek in Belgium.

(Stuart Emery collection)

This splendid view of the steam tug **Contest** was taken off Gravesend in 1971 with Tilbury A and B power stations evident in the background. The **Contest** was completed in March 1933 by Alexander Hall & Co Ltd of Aberdeen and her machinery consisted of a 1100ihp triple expansion steam engine. She was delivered to her owner Elliott Steam Tug Company Ltd, London, and was managed by J Page. She was similar to Elliott's **Challenge** of 1931, and was actually built as a replacement for the previous tug named **Contest** completed in 1931, which had been sold to Italian owners in 1932. Built as a coal-burning tug, she was converted to oil-burning on Tyneside in 1958. As part of the Ship Towage fleet since 1950, her ownership changed from Elliott Steam Tug Company Ltd to William Watkins Ltd in 1965. The **Contest** became part of the newly created London Tugs Ltd in 1969, and following boiler trouble, she was towed to shipbreakers T W Ward at Grays on 7 April 1972, by her sister tug **Challenge**.

(The late C C Beazley)

On 1 February 1950 the tug fleets of William Watkins Ltd and The Elliott Steam Tug Co (1949) Ltd were amalgamated to form Ship Towage (London) Ltd which then took control of Gamecock Tugs Ltd (previously Gamecock Steam Towing). However the tugs continued to wear the funnel colours of their previous owners. The *Crested Cock* was completed in 1935 by Alexander Hall & Co Ltd at Aberdeen and was delivered to Gamecock Steam Towing Co Ltd, London. Like the similar 1932-built *Ocean Cock* and

Atlantic Cock, the *Crested Cock* had a triple expansion steam engine with an indicated horse power of 900. In 1950 her owner became William Watkins Ltd, with Ship Towage (London) Ltd as her managers and she was later absorbed into London Tugs Ltd in 1969. This view of her in the King George V lock dates from 1968. The *Crested Cock* was sold in early 1970 to shipbreakers at Antwerp together with the *Atlantic Cock*.

(The late C C Beazley)

The **Napia** was completed in July 1943 by Goole Shipbuilding & Repairing Co Ltd as **Empire Jester** for the Ministry of War Transport. In June 1944 she took part in the Normandy landings and was sold to William Watkins Ltd, London, in 1946, and renamed **Napia**. In 1950 her managers became Ship Towage (London) Ltd and in 1965 she gained the new Ship Towage funnel markings. This was based on the William Watkins colours of black with a broad red band which now bore the Elliott Steam Tug Company's "Dick and Page" house flag. The narrow blue band seen in this view of the **Napia** was the same shade as previously used on the funnels of the Gamecock tugs fleet within Ship Towage (London) Ltd. The **Napia** duly passed to London Tugs Ltd in the amalgamation of 1969. She was withdrawn in 1971 and sold to Greek owners John G Efthimou of Piraeus as **Tolmiros**. In 1973 she passed to Loucas G Matsas, also at Piraeus, and was eventually scrapped at Perama in early 1986.

(The late C C Beazley)

In 2016 the **Cervia** is probably the last surviving Empire-type steam tug in the northern hemisphere. She was launched on 21 January 1946 at the yard of Alexander Hall & Co, Aberdeen, as **Empire Raymond** and was delivered to Ministry of War Transport. She was purchased in December the same year by William Watkins Ltd, London, and renamed **Cervia** in 1947. She was powered by a 700ihp triple expansion steam engine and had an overall length of 112 feet. At Tilbury on 25 October 1954, she was girted while attached to the passenger ship **Arcadia**, and sank with the loss of five lives.

However she was raised and put back into service. In this view of her dating from early 1971, she is operating for London Tugs Ltd. By May of the same year, the **Cervia** was laid up and later sold, initially for preservation, but soon put back into commercial use until about 1983. In 1984 she went on permanent loan to the East Kent Maritime Museum at Ramsgate. In 2013 the **Cervia** received a grant towards her cosmetic restoration and then re-opened to the public.

(The late C C Beazley)

The Tilbury Contracting & Dredging Co Ltd was engaged in towing hopper barges of dredged spoil from London's docklands to dumping grounds in the Thames estuary, and during WWII the company was to be found working around the UK coast as well as on French contracts. In 1937 Cochrane & Sons Ltd of Selby constructed the two large steam tugs *Danube V* and *Danube VI* for Tilbury Contracting & Dredging and followed this in May 1946 with a pair of similar tugs, *Danube VII* and her sistership *Danube VIII*. They had oil-fired boilers providing steam for a 900ihp triple expansion engine constructed by Charles D Holmes & Co Ltd of Hull. In 1965 the operations of Tilbury Contracting & Dredging Co Ltd were merged with Westminster Dredging Co Ltd, London. It is in Westminster's colours that we see the *Danube VII* in this photograph. The *Danube VII* was sold in 1969 to Italian owners Società Anonima Italiani Lavori Edili Marittimi of Palermo, and was renamed *Giove Sailem*. She was eventually broken up at Palermo in late 1984.

(Stuart Emery collection)

At the end of WWII a number of Foremost class Empire-type tugs were in various stages of build at Alexander Hall's yard at Aberdeen. Two of these, the *Empire Leonard* and *Empire Margaret*, had been launched for the Ministry of Transport, but were then sold for £33,000 each to W H J Alexander Ltd, London. They were renamed *Sun XVI* and *Sun XVII* and completed in September and November 1946 respectively. These fine-looking tugs had a gross tonnage of 233 and were powered by a 700ihp Alexander Hall triple expansion steam engine. In 1962 the *Sun XVI* was sold to Società Rimorchiatori Napoletani, Naples, and renamed *San Cataldo*. The *Sun XVII* continued to work on the Thames and we see her in June 1967 working as the stern tug on Pacific Steam Navigation's *Salamanca*. In 1968 the *Sun XVII* joined her sister with the same Italian owner and took the name *Rania G.* In June 1983 she was broken up at Palermo in Sicily.

(Stuart Emery collection)

When delivered to W H J Alexander Ltd, London, in February 1951, the *Sun XVIII* was the first of seven motor tugs for her owner to be completed by Philip & Son Ltd at Dartmouth. She was a relatively small ship-handling tug at 105grt and was intended for use serving the upriver enclosed docks. The *Sun XVIII* had an overall length of 88 feet and was powered by a 7-cyl Vickers Armstrong-built Ruston & Hornsby diesel of 560bhp. On this occasion she is seen in the King George V entrance lock in 1968.

(The late C C Beazley)

The *Sun XVIII* passed to London Tugs Ltd in 1969 and is seen in August 1971 in their colours underway on the Thames. The following year she moved to Felixstowe and spent a period on charter to Gaselee. When London Tugs was taken over by Alexandra Towing Co Ltd on 1 January 1975, the *Sun XVIII* returned to the Thames and was soon sold, passing to London-based A & N Vogel Ltd, and changing her name to *Ecclesbourne*. Two years later she was sold to Greek owner General Hellas Ltd, and registered at Piraeus as *Alexandros*. From 1981 she was registered at Kerkyra (Corfu) for Petros & Spyridon Rarakos and was laid up at Corfu by 1997, subsequently falling into a state of dereliction within 5 years of this.

(Paul Andow collection)

In many ways similar to the *Fossa* (page 49) was the older *Rana* of 1951. She was completed by Cochrane & Sons Ltd at Selby and delivered to Gaselee & Son Ltd, London. She had a gross tonnage of 98 and her main engine was a 5-cyl British Polar diesel developing 750bhp. The *Rana* like the other Gaselee motor tugs was completed with a tall funnel resembling that of a steam tug. The *Rana* received a smaller funnel after passing to Ship Towage (London) Ltd in 1965. In this 1970 view she is in London Tugs Ltd colours in the vicinity of the King George V lock.

The *Rana* briefly operated at Felixstowe in 1974, and upon passing to Alexandra Towing Co Ltd in 1975, was transferred to Swansea. She was sold in 1978 passing to Humphrey & Grey (Lighterage) Ltd, London, as *Redriff*. In 1984 she joined the fleet of Alan C Bennett & Sons Ltd and received the name *Rana* once again. In 2002 she was sold, becoming a houseboat in Hoo Marina, where she was still based in 2013.

(The late C C Beazley)

The **Plangent** and **Plagal** were the first of four modern 1200bhp twin-screw tugs completed for the Port of London Authority (PLA), and intended for use in the Royal Docks. The **Plangent** was delivered to her owners in December 1951 from her builder Henry Scarr Ltd at Hessle. She had a gross tonnage of 159 and an overall length of 92 feet. She was powered by a pair of 4-cyl Crossley diesels, and in 1968 these were replaced by two Lister Blackstone diesels. In 1972 the **Plangent** struck an obstruction in the King George V lock and sank shortly afterwards. She was raised and put back into use as seen here in this view from 3 June 1973. She was eventually transferred to the PLA dredging unit and was sold in 1986 to Greek owner Hellenic Tugs who renamed her **Cerberus**. By 1997 she was with Kerveros Naftiki Eteria, also of Piraeus, and named **Kerveros**. It is thought she was still in service up until 2006.

(The late C C Beazley)

The second pair of tugs in the quartet bore the names **Platina** and **Plateau** and were similar in most respects to the **Plangent** and **Plagal**. The **Plateau** was however fitted with a pair of Kort nozzles from new. The **Platina** was delivered in May 1952 and was usually to be found working the Royal Docks until about 1966. Following the delivery of the four new Voith Schneider tractor tugs, these tugs then worked the West India dock, and also at Tilbury. The continued downturn in trade on the Thames saw the **Platina** and **Plateau** sold to Holyhead Towing Co Ltd in 1973. The **Platina** was renamed **Afon Goch** and later **Afon Caradoc** in 1976, but was only ever used as a source of parts for her sister **Plateau** which served Holyhead Towing for many years as **Afon Las**. The former **Platina** was broken up in the Netherlands in 1979.

(The late C C Beazley)

The impressive looking tug *Vanquisher* was completed by Henry Scarr Ltd at Hessle and delivered to her owners The Elliott Steam Tug Co (1949) Ltd in March 1955. At 1280bhp, she was the most powerful single-screw tug in service on the River Thames, and the first diesel tug in the Ship Towage fleet. In 1965 her ownership transferred to William Watkins Ltd, and she was managed by Ship Towage (London) Ltd. In 1966 the *Vanquisher* gained certification to carry 100 passengers, while in the early 1970s her main engine was converted to bridge control. She became part of the London Tugs Ltd fleet in 1969 which was taken over by Alexandra Towing in 1975. Whilst undocking the container ship *Jervis Bay* from Tilbury on 8 January 1976, the *Vanquisher* was girted and quickly sank. Thankfully all of her crew were picked up safely. She was later raised and placed back in service at Gravesend six months later. She finally bowed out in June 1982, having been replaced by the modern tractor tug *Sun Thames*. The *Vanquisher* was towed away for breaking up at Bloors Wharf, Rainham, Kent.

(The late C C Beazley)

The **Sun XIX** of 1956 and her sister **Sun XX** of 1957 were completed at the South Devon yard of Philip & Son Ltd at Dartmouth for W H J Alexander Ltd, London. They were equipped with limited fire-fighting capability and also had a salvage pump. In addition they each had DTI certification for 27 passengers. Unlike the final pair of tugs in this quartet, the **Sun XIX** and **Sun XX** were each completed with a pair of lifeboats. The **Sun XIX** had a gross tonnage of 192 and was powered by an 1170bhp Ruston & Hornsby diesel engine. In this view the **Sun XIX** is in the colours of London Tugs Ltd, ending her days on the Thames in the ownership of Alexandra Towing Co Ltd. The **Sun XIX** was sold in 1979 to Italian owner Società Rimorchiatori Napoletani, Naples, becoming **Sole Primo**. She was broken up at Aliaga, Turkey in 1996.

(The late C C Beazley)

On 1 January 1975, the Alexandra Towing Co Ltd of Liverpool took over the operations of London Tugs Ltd, Gaselee & Son (Felixstowe) Ltd and The Medway Dry Dock & Engineering Co Ltd, Sheerness. From this Alexandra Towing Co (London) Ltd was thus formed and the deal involved 23 tugs. The **Sun XX** was delivered to W H J Alexander Ltd in May 1957 and her Ruston & Hornsby diesel gave her a speed of 12 knots. This view of her dates from July 1976 and demonstrates how well many of the vessels in the takeover looked upon gaining the colours of Alexandra Towing. Like her sister **Sun XIX**, the **Sun XX** also passed to Italian owner Società Rimorchiatori Napoletani, of Naples where her name was changed to **Sole Secondo**. She too was broken up in Turkey during 1996.

(Andrew Wiltshire collection)

On 1 May 1965 Ship Towage (London) Ltd took over the tugs **Fossa**, **Rana**, **Culex** and **Vespa** from Gaselee and Son Ltd. With this deal came a number of ship handling contracts, including one for all ships visiting Bowater's paper mill at Ridham Dock in Kent. Initially both the **Culex** and **Fossa** received Watkins' funnel markings of black with a broad red band. Of the four tugs the **Culex** was the odd one out being completed at a West German shipyard. She was constructed by F Schichau AG, Bremerhaven in 1958 and delivered to Gaselee & Son Ltd fitted with a tall, hinged steam tug shape funnel. The **Culex** had a gross tonnage of 97 and was powered by a 660bhp Deutz diesel. Her funnel was removed later in 1965 and replaced by a smaller design as visible in this photograph. She was transferred to London Tugs Ltd in 1969 and sold to Greek owners in 1971. Registered at Piraeus she was renamed **Atromitos** for service with John G Efthimiou. It is thought she was still active at Volos in Greek waters as recently as 2010. By then she boasted a new Caterpillar engine and a more modern wheelhouse.

(The late C C Beazley)

The **Dhulia** was the first of two similar motor tugs added to the Ship Towage (London) Ltd fleet in 1959 and stationed at Gravesend. She was completed by Henry Scar Ltd , Hessle, and was owned by William Watkins Ltd. She had a limited fire-fighting capability, and along with her sister **Moorcock**, was capable of pumping either water or foam. We see the **Dhulia** in action just outside the Royal docks in the livery of London Tugs Ltd, and by this time her main engine may well have been converted to bridge control. She joined the Alexandra Towing Co (London) Ltd fleet in 1975, and after a spell working at Great Yarmouth in 1980 was based at Felixstowe by early 1982. She was sold in April 1983 to Chara SA, and renamed **Dhulia S**. under the Panamanian flag. It is not known if she ever operated as such, and was eventually broken up in late 1985 at Hendrik-ido-Ambacht in the Netherlands.

(The late C C Beazley)

This dramatic shot of the **Moorcock** in Alexandra Towing colours was taken in the autumn of 1978. She was completed by Henry Scarr Ltd of Hessle with a gross tonnage of 272 and was then delivered to Gamecock Tugs Ltd, in October 1959, being managed by Ship Towage (London) Ltd. Her main engine was an 8-cyl direct-acting British Polar diesel of 1600bhp, which gave the **Moorcock** a speed of 12 knots. In 1981 she was replaced at Gravesend by the secondhand tractor tug **Sun Swale**. The **Moorcock** was stripped of all useful parts and towed away to Queenborough by the tug **Watercock** for breaking up.

(The late John Wiltshire collection)

The **Sun XXII** was the sister vessel to the **Sun XXI** on the cover of this book. She was delivered in February 1960, the final tug in the quartet from Philip & Son Ltd at Dartmouth. In 1969 she passed to London Tugs Ltd in whose colours she is seen here just off the entrance to the King Geroge V lock in 1970. In 1975 London Tugs Ltd passed to Alexandra Towing Co (London) Ltd. The **Sun XXII** was then transferred to the Felixstowe fleet, and in early 1976 was renamed **Deben.** She briefly moved to Swansea and then sailed out to Gibraltar in December 1978 as the inaugural tug at Alexandra's new base in the port. She was disposed of in 1986 initially passing to Atlantic Shipping Company before moving to the Isle of Man flag for Dringburn Ltd. This all proved to be short lived as she became stranded and later sank off the South Moroccan coast.

(The late C C Beazley)

The *Ionia* was another motor tug completed by Henry Scarr Ltd for service on the Thames. She was delivered in August 1960 to William Watkins Ltd, London, and was intended for station at Ship Towage's Woolwich base. In 1973 the *Ionia* had a Towmaster nozzle fitted and this increased her bollard pull to 22 tonnes. She continued to serve on the Thames with Alexandra Towing Co Ltd, as seen in this view off Gravesend on 3 April 1982, with spells at Felixstowe and Southampton. The *Ionia* was then sold to Falmouth Towage Co Ltd in late 1987 and worked at this Cornish port as *St. Mawes* until 2001. At this point she was sold and returned to the River Thames area for further service which did not materialise and she was laid up. By 2005 she had moved to a berth at Bideford in North Devon and carried the name *Ionia* once again. Her condition continued to deteriorate, and in 2009 she was sold to Rachael Swain, Bideford, for conversion into a floating café to be called 'Tea on the Tug'. As far as is known this never took place and the *Ionia* remains at Bideford awaiting her fate.

(Danny Lynch)

From 1879 Charles Gaselee built up a fleet of tugs for towing barges between the Royal Albert Dock and upriver wharves. Gaselee also entered into ship-handling and the first diesel tug *Adoma* arrived in 1933. Gaselee and Son Ltd was formed in 1935, and many more motor tugs were acquired. The *Fossa* was delivered from Henry Scarr Ltd at Hessle in 1961. She was powered by an 8-cyl Deutz diesel with an output of 1000bhp. Upon passing to Ship Towage (London) Ltd in 1965, the *Fossa* went on to receive a smaller motor tug style funnel. She passed to London Tugs Ltd in 1969 in whose colours we see her in this 1970 view. She then passed to Alexandra Towing Co Ltd in 1975 and was replaced by the *Sun Essex* in 1977. She was sold to Darling Bros Ltd, London, as *Kilda*, and later operated for Alan C Bennett & Sons Ltd, Rochester, as *Mamba* between 1987 and 2002. She then became a houseboat at Port Werburgh, and following a change of owner, from 2016 was relocated to Hoo Marina on the Medway.

(The late C C Beazley)

The motor tug **Sun XXIII** was delivered to W H J Alexander in March 1961 and allocated to their upriver fleet. She was completed by Philip & Son Ltd at Dartmouth and was powered by a 6-cyl Mirrlees diesel developing 1080bhp. In 1969 she passed to London Tugs Ltd and then in 1975 to Alexandra Towing Co Ltd. The **Sun XXIII** was eventually sold to Guernsey-based Havelet International Ltd in 1984 and renamed **Sunwind**, returning to the Thames the following year as **Suncrest** for S & H Towage. She had other owners in the London area before passing to General Marine Services Ltd in 1990. She was put up for sale in 2004 and remained laid up in 2016. In this 1968 view the **Sun XXIII** is wearing the colours of her original owner W H J Alexander.

(The late C C Beazley)

This shot of the **Avenger** was taken in January 1963 when the tug was barely two months old. She was the first of a pair of fire-fighting tugs completed by Cochrane & Sons Ltd, Selby, for operation in the Ship Towage (London) Ltd fleet. She was delivered in November 1962 in the colours of The Elliott Steam Tug Co (1949) Ltd, and by the end of the year her owner was quoted as William Watkins Ltd, London. As can be seen, the **Avenger** has a very prominent tripod mast with fire-fighting platform and was capable of delivering either water or foam. In 1965 she received the funnel markings of Ship Towage (London) Ltd and in 1969 was merged into the London Tugs Ltd fleet. In 1974 she was sent to a shipyard on the Tyne to have a controllable-pitch propeller and a Towmaster nozzle fitted. As a result of this, upon her return to the Thames in 1975, her bollard pull had risen from 18 to 32 tonnes. The **Avenger** then served in the Alexandra Towing Co (London) Ltd fleet for ten years until 1985, when she was sold to Purvis Marine Ltd, Sault Ste Marie, Ontario. She became **Avenger IV** under the Canadian flag and was still in service on the Great Lakes in 2016.

(Stuart Emery collection)

The **Hibernia** was the sister tug to the **Avenger** and was delivered from Cochrane's in January 1963. She was owned by William Watkins Ltd and managed by Ship Towage (London) Ltd. She is seen here in June 1965 in Watkins colours. Like the **Avenger**, the **Hibernia** had a gross tonnage of 293 and an overall length of 118 feet. Her main engine was a 9-cyl British Polar diesel of 1800bhp which gave her a speed 12 knots. Again like the **Avenger**, the **Hibernia** had her propulsion system upgraded, and in 1975 was sent to Sheerness to receive a controllable-pitch propeller and a Towmaster nozzle. She ended her days on the Thames working for Alexandra Towing Co (London) Ltd from 1975 until 1987.

(Stuart Emery collection)

This superb shot of the *Hibernia* was taken off Gravesend in June 1985 and shows very clearly her fire-fighting gear located on the specially designed mast structure. She was also fitted with a salvage pump. The *Hibernia* and her sister *Avenger* were intended for service at Gravesend as well as serving the oil terminals at Isle of Grain and Shell Haven. The *Hibernia* was sold in 1987 to Greek owners, and initially became *Atrotos* for Achilleus II Shipping Co, Thessaloniki. After a number of subsequent owners, she is still very recognisable as the former *Hibernia* in 2015, bearing the name *Alfios*, and working for Ergasies Rimoulkiseos Katakolou Naftiki Eteria registered in Piraeus.

(Paul Andow)

The *Sun XXIV* is noted off the King George V lock in October 1975, the year of the Alexandra Towing takeover. She was another of the smaller tugs built for W H J Alexander Ltd (Sun Tugs), for use in the vicinity of the upriver docks. She was the first motor tug for this fleet from the yard of James Pollock Sons & Co, Faversham, and was delivered in June 1962. She had a gross tonnage of 113 and an overall length of 88 feet. The *Sun XXIV* was transferred to Southampton in 1979 and eventually sold by Alexandra Towing in 1990, passing to Sub Search Marine Services Ltd, Newhaven. In 1992 she became *Kingston*, and subsequently led a varied and sometimes dubious career with a number of different fleets mainly in the south of England. By 2003 she was with Griffin Towage & Marine (J A Eveleigh), London, who in 2005 fitted a bow thruster and a Kort nozzle to the vessel. She was still in service in 2016.

(The late C C Beazley)

The **Sun XXV** was delivered to W H J Alexander Ltd in January 1963 and was the last ship-handling tug completed by Philip & Son Ltd at Dartmouth. She was a fire-fighting tug of 230 tons gross and had an overall length of 116 feet. She was powered by a 1810bhp Mirrlees Blackstone diesel and had a speed of 12 knots. Following a brief spell working at Felixstowe in 1967, she passed to London Tugs Ltd in 1969, and then Alexandra Towing Co (London) Ltd in 1975. She was one of the three remaining former Sun tugs to pass with the Alexandra Towing business to Howard Smith Towage Ltd on 1 March 1993. In 1997 the **Sun XXV** was sold to Taipan Shipping Ltd of Trinidad, and renamed **Saga Star** under the Belize flag. She was then towed to the Caribbean by the tug **Saga Moon** (formerly **Sun XXVI**). She passed to Saint Vincent Tugs & Salvage Ltd, Kingstown, in 2004, but had been scrapped by 2011.

(The late C C Beazley)

Alan C Bennett began trading in 1983 and provided towing contracts for a number of civil engineering and dredging projects in the Thames area. His company eventually established a link with aggregates producer Foster Yeoman. The *Argonaut* was a former Dutch tug that was operated by Alan C Bennett & Sons Ltd of Rochester. She was built in the Netherlands by Scheepswerven v/h H H Bodewes at Millingen, and was delivered in July 1963 to L Smit & Co's Internationale Sleepdienst Mij N.V. of Rotterdam as *Argonaut*. The following year they received a similar tug *Astronaut*. The *Argonaut* passed to Alan Bennett in 1989 as the *Argonaut-B*. She regained her original name *Argonaut* in about 2000 and by 2011 was put into lay-up. She was broken up at Northfleet in 2013.

(Ian Willett)

The livery used by the Alexandra Towing Company suited most traditional tugs and the *Sun II* is no exception. She is seen off Gravesend on 26 August 1976 with Tilbury docks in the background. She was completed in 1965 by Charles D Holmes at Hull and delivered to W H J Alexander Ltd. She was intended for use in the upriver fleet serving the West India and Royal docks. The *Sun II* had a gross tonnage of 150 and her main engine was a 6-cyl Mirrlees National of 1400bhp. She remained based on the Thames for 27 years, and in 1992 was sold by Alexandra Towing Company to Greek owners. She was duly renamed *Alexandros* for Vergina Towing Co Ltd, Chalkis, and is still at work in 2017.

(The late C C Beazley)

The **Sun XXVI** was a similar tug to the **Sun XXV** of 1963, and was the first of two tugs completed for W H J Alexander Ltd by the Yorkshire shipyard of Charles D Holmes & Co Ltd, Beverley. She was delivered in March 1965 and was a fire-fighting tug based at Gravesend. The **Sun XXVI** had a gross tonnage of 230 and an overall length of 116 feet. Her main engine was a 6-cyl Mirrlees KLSSDM-6 which developed 1810bhp. In 1969 she was absorbed into the newly-created fleet of London Tugs Ltd, and this is how we see her in this 1971 view near Gravesend. In 1975 she passed to Alexandra Towing Co (London) Ltd, and in 1978 was fitted with a Kort nozzle and three small rudders which increased her bollard pull from 22 to 35 tonnes. The **Sun XXVI** continued to work for Howard Smith Towage Ltd from 1993 until her sale in 1997 to Saga Shipping Ltd, St Nevis. She was renamed **Saga Moon** under the Belize flag. She was believed to be still active in 2017 with Saint Vincent Tugs & Salvage Ltd, Kingstown.

(The late C C Beazley)

The **Sun III** was very similar to the **Sun II** (see page 54) being delivered a year later in 1966. The **Sun III** was however completed at Faversham by James Pollock Sons & Co, and was powered by a slightly less powerful Mirrlees diesel, which gave her a speed of 12 knots. In this 1968 view of the **Sun III** we see her acting as bow tug on a freighter inbound to the Royal Docks. Passing to London Tugs Ltd in 1969 and then Alexandra Towing

Co (London) Ltd in 1975, the **Sun III** was transferred to Swansea in 1984. Here she acquired the local name **Fabian's Bay** and was re-registered at that port. She joined her sister ship **Sun II** once more in October 1992 when she was sold for further service in Greece with Vergina Towing Co Ltd, at Chalkis. They renamed her **Filippos**, and as such, she was still in service in 2014.

(The late C C Beazley)

A familiar sight for many years was the sight of ship-handling tugs moored on the buoys off Gravesend. In this view taken on 22 August 1984 we see a group of three fire-fighting tugs awaiting their next turn of duty. In the centre is the *Avenger* (see page 51) which dates from 1962. She is flanked by her sister-ship the *Hibernia* (see pages 51 and 52), and *Sun XXVI* of 1965 (page 55). During the 1970s all three of these tugs could at times be found engaged on coastal towing duties around the UK coast. The *Avenger* and *Hibernia* were nearing the end of their working lives on the Thames as modern Voith Schneider tractor tugs were gradually introduced to the Gravesend fleet.

(Paul Andow)

The last new ship-handling tugs delivered to the Port of London Authority were four highly-manoeuvrable Voith Schneider tractors in 1965/66. They were initially intended for use within the Royal Docks but eventually ended up working out of Tilbury. Here we see one of them in action. The *Plasma* of 1965 is photographed in April 1969 out on the River Thames at the lock entrance to the King George V dock. She was completed by Richard Dunston (Hessle) Ltd with an overall length of 87 feet. She had a single Voith Schneider propulsion unit mounted forward of amidships, and as can clearly be seen in this view her towing hook was situated well aft. When the PLA sold off their last dock system at Tilbury in 1991 the *Plasma* was sold to Alexandra Towing Co Ltd, Gravesend, becoming *Burma* and based at Gravesend (see page 68).

`(The late John Wiltshire collection)`

The **Platoon** was the first of the quartet, being delivered to the PLA from Richard Dunston Ltd, Hessle, in February 1965. The last two tugs in this series were named **Plankton** and **Placard** and all four were powered by a 16-cyl Lister Blackstone diesel of 1600bhp which gave them a bollard pull of 16 tonnes. This view of the **Platoon** shows to good effect her round-fronted superstructure, reminiscent of the Port of Antwerp Authority Voith tractors from the early 1960s. The **Platoon** followed the **Plasma** to Alexandra Towing Co Ltd becoming **Dhulia** (see page 68).

(Andrew Wiltshire collection)

On 1 January 1991 the Port of London Authority reduced its last remaining dock towage fleet, based at Tilbury, from four to two tugs, the **Placard** and **Plankton**. One would normally be kept as a spare tug and dock towage at Tilbury was supplemented with vessels from the Alexandra Towing Co fleet based at Gravesend. In September 1991 the **Placard** and **Plankton** passed to the new owner of Tilbury dock, Port of Tilbury London Ltd. They were renamed **Orsett** and **Linford** after nearby villages. They are seen moored in Tilbury dock in early 1992. This arrangement continued until 1998 when the two tugs were sold to Deans Tugs & Workboats Ltd, Hull, retaining their names. The **Orsett** was out of action by 2002 and is thought to have been used as a source of spare parts, until broken up in 2013. The **Linford** is thought to be still in existence in 2016.

(Stuart Emery)

The **Watercock** was completed by Richard Dunston (Hessle) Ltd, Hessle, and delivered to Ship Towage (London) Ltd in June 1967. She had an overall length of 100 feet and her 1050bhp Ruston and Hornsby diesel engine gave her a speed of 12¼ knots. Following the takeover of Ship Towage (London) Ltd by London Tugs Ltd in January 1969, her primitive open wheelhouse was replaced by an enclosed structure. This was manufactured using fibre glass and can be seen to good effect in this view taken from the landing stage at Gravesend in 1971. The **Watercock** continued to serve on the Thames after passing into the ownership of Alexandra Towing Co (London) Ltd on 1 January 1975. On 19 November 1989 she was towed away by the **Sun London** for breaking up by the Medway Dry Dock Co, Sheerness.

(The late C C Beazley)

The **Burma** was the sister to the **Watercock**. She was also completed on Humberside by Richard Dunston (Hessle) Ltd and delivered in February 1967. Her registered owner was William Watkins Ltd, and she was allocated to the Woolwich tug base. The **Burma** was of outdated appearance in that she had an open wheelhouse reminiscent of 1930s era Thames tugs. In place of a conventional lifeboat she had an inflatable liferaft. In this view dating from 1968, the **Burma** is seen in original condition in the King George V lock on the stern of the Ben Line cargo ship **Benratha**. She passed to the London Tugs Ltd fleet in 1969 and eventually received an enclosed wheelhouse. From 1975 she was operating for the Alexandra Towing Co (London) Ltd, latterly based at Gravesend. In 1989, the **Burma** was stripped of useful parts by The Medway Dry Dock & Engineering Co at Sheerness, and then broken up.

(The late C C Beazley)

Delivered in December 1968, the **Sun XXVII** was the last new tug to be ordered by W H J Alexander Ltd, and in effect at 226grt, a larger and more powerful development of the **Sun XIX** of 1956. There were in total seven tugs built with this distinctive outline, the **Sun XXVII** having a prominent fire-fighting platform on her mast, as well as boasting a much larger funnel. The **Sun XXVII** was one of the last tugs completed by James Pollock Sons & Co Ltd at Faversham, and passed to London Tugs Ltd when barely a month old. By the time she passed into the Alexandra Towing Co (London) Ltd fleet in 1975, her gross tonnage was recorded as 249grt. From 1993 she was part of the Howard Smith Towage fleet on the Thames. The **Sun XXVII** was sold to Taipan Shipping Ltd of Trinidad in 1997 and took the new name **Saga Sun**, sailing under the Belize flag. By 2003 she was with Mariners Haven Ltd also of Trinidad and was still in service in 2015.

(The late John Wiltshire collection)

The first Voith Schneider ship-handling tug on the Thames was the **Sun Swale**. She was purchased secondhand in September 1981 from the French tug operator Soc. de Remorquage et de Sauvetage du Nord. She was previously the **Clairvoyant**, and was based at Dunkerque. She had been completed in 1968 by Ziegler Frères, Dunkerque, and had a 1400bhp Crepelle diesel driving a single Voith Schneider propulsion unit. The **Sun Swale** was fitted for fire-fighting and was initially stationed at Gravesend, but moved to Ramsgate in 1985. She was then transferred to Gibraltar in 1990, passing into ownership of Howard Smith Towage Ltd in March 1993. In 1998 she was sold to T P Towage Co Ltd of Gibraltar for further service. The **Sun Swale** was sunk on 16 March 2015 in 22 metres of water off the South Mole, as part of Gibraltar's artificial reef project.

(Andrew Wiltshire collection)

By 15 August 1991, the Gravesend fleet was made up of eight Voith tractors and nine conventional screw tugs. The *Agile* and *Adept* were also of French origin and completed as *Agile* and *Alerte* respectively by Ziegler Frères, Dunkerque, in 1971. They were single-unit Voith tractors and came to the UK in 1978 when purchased by Alexandra Towing Co Ltd for use in the Bulk Cargo Handling Services Ltd fleet based at Liverpool. In 1986 they transferred into the main Alexandra Towing Co Ltd fleet and arrived at Gravesend in September 1988. They spent periods handling barges at Coryton and the Canary Wharf project. In 1993 they were included in the Howard Smith takeover of Alexandra Towing. The *Agile* and *Adept* were eventually based at Grimsby from 1994, and were then sold in 1997 to Bilberry Shipping & Stevedoring Co Ltd of Waterford, Eire. In 2016 they were working for Fastnet Shipping, Waterford.

(The late John Wiltshire)

The *Hendon* spent 11 years as part of the Gravesend-based fleet, arriving there from Southampton in 1985. This view of her dates from 20 August 1992. She was built in 1977 by Richard Dunston (Hessle), Hessle, for the account of France Fenwick Tyne & Wear Co Ltd at Newcastle, who were unable to take delivery. Her sister ship was *Cragsider*. The *Hendon* was then sold to Alexandra Towing Co Ltd, Liverpool, in 1978 and allocated to the Swansea fleet for harbour and coastal towing. She was a powerful tug with a 6-cyl Mirrlees Blackstone diesel of 3226bhp giving her an impressive bollard pull of 46 tonnes. Upon arrival at Gravesend her towing winch was repositioned. The *Hendon* left British waters in 1996 for a new career with Karapiperis 12 Naftiki Eteria, Piraeus, as *Karapiperis 12* under the Greek flag. By 2015 she was sailing under the Greek flag as *Ethy VI*.

(Stuart Emery)

The first new tugs for Alexandra Towing Company's Gravesend fleet were three ordered for delivery in 1977 from Richard Dunston (Hessle) Ltd. The second of these was the **Sun Kent** which was delivered in October 1977. The **Sun Kent** had a gross tonnage of 272 and featured a controllable-pitch propeller in a steerable Kort nozzle. In 1993 she passed with the Alexandra Towing business to Howard Smith Towage Ltd, in whose livery we see her on 20 April 1996 near Northfleet. She was sold by Howard Smith in 1999 passing to Rebonave, Setubal, and sailed under the Portuguese flag. In 2000 she moved to Lisbontugs - Companhia de Rebocadores de Lisboa S A and took the new name **Montabo**. This name was then altered to **Montado** in 2001. After several changes of flag and ownership, in 2013 the former **Sun Kent** was sailing as the **Sharon 1** under the Cook Islands flag.

(Ian Willett)

The **Sun Essex** was the first of the new tugs delivered from Richard Dunston in 1977, and is seen here underway at Northfleet on 5 May 1989. She was a powerful fire-fighting tug with a bollard pull of around 35 tonnes and was powered by a 12-cyl Ruston diesel engine. The final tug in the trio was the **Sun London** which arrived on the Thames in November 1977, and was slightly different having a bollard pull of 45 tonnes and was not fitted for fire-fighting. The **Sun Essex** was transferred to Southampton in January 1990 passing to Howard Smith Towage Ltd in 1993. She was sold in 1999 passing to Norwegian owner Arne Nilsen Slepebåter A/S as the **Big**. In 2002 her name changed once again when she became the **Susanne A**. and in 2007 the **Lucas** for Danish owners. By 2012 she was sailing under the Belize flag for Dutch owner Sovlot BV of Zwijndrecht, and had regained her original name **Sun Essex**.

(Ian Willett)

The large twin-screw tugs **Formidable** and her sister **Indomitable** were delivered to Alexandra Towing Co Ltd for coastal and overseas towing duties. Both were completed in 1979 by Richard Dunston (Hessle) Ltd. The **Formidable** followed her sister into service and was based at Gravesend from new. She had a gross tonnage of 406 and a very impressive bollard pull of 55 tonnes. Her controllable-pitch propellers were installed in Kort nozzles, and she also featured a bow thruster. She is seen here in June 1985. In March 1993 she passed from Alexandra Towing to Howard Smith Towage, and on to Adsteam (UK) Ltd in 1999, The **Formidable** eventually left UK waters in 2001. She was sold to Danish owner Niels Henriksen, who renamed her **Eurosund**. By 2012 she was sailing under the flag of Sierra Leone as **Mignon**, with her owner named as Kiev Shipping & Trading.

(Paul Andow)

Having been purpose built for use in Alexandra Towing Company's Felixstowe fleet, the *Ganges* transferred to Gravesend in 1993 following the Howard Smith Towage takeover. The *Ganges* was the final conventional single-screw motor tug delivered to Alexandra, and was completed in May 1982 by Richard Dunston at Hessle. She had a bollard pull of 39 tonnes and her main power unit was a 12-cyl Ruston diesel of 2640bhp, driving a controllable-pitch propeller in a steerable Kort nozzle. Being a fire-fighting tug, she was a useful vessel to have allocated to the Thames. Here we see the *Ganges* in Howard Smith colours off Gravesend on 8 April 1997. She was absorbed into Adsteam (UK) Ltd in 1999 and sold to the Londonderry Port and Harbour Commissioners in 2005. Here she was renamed *Culmore* and later fitted with a directional bow thruster unit. She was still a spare tug at Londonderry in 2017.

(Stuart Emery)

The *Sun Thames* was the first new tug with twin Voith Schneider propulsion units acquired for the Gravesend fleet of Alexandra Towing Co Ltd. She was from the yard of McTay Marine Ltd, Bromborough and was delivered in May 1982 to replace the *Vanquisher* (page 44). The *Sun Thames* had a bollard pull of 30 tonnes and was fitted for fire-fighting with three monitors capable of delivering either water or foam as required. This view of her is from June 1985 and shows her passing Gravesend while attending a container vessel.

(Paul Andow)

The **Sun Thames** continued to work at Gravesend passing into Howard Smith Towage Ltd ownership from 1993. The Adsteam (UK) Ltd takeover of Howard Smith Towage in 1999 saw her gain the colours depicted in this image, taken in Tilbury lock on 17 April 2004. In 2006 the **Sun Thames** was transferred to Humber Tugs Ltd, based at Hull, and renamed **HT Sword**.

Humber Tugs Ltd was established to provide a low cost towage operation on the Humber. The Adsteam group passed to Svitzer Marine Ltd in 2007 and the **HT Sword** was renamed **Svitzer Sword**. She was then sold to Romanian owners in 2010 as **BSV Anglia**.

(Ian Willett)

As mentioned previously, in 1991 the Port of London Authority reduced its ship-handling dock tugs fleet to two vessels and disposed of the **Plasma** and **Platoon**. Despite their age, these useful tugs were sold to Alexandra Towing Co and sent to Sheerness for an overhaul. They re-entered service as part of the Gravesend-based fleet bearing the traditional names **Burma** and **Dhulia** respectively. This photograph was taken on 15 August 1991 with the sisters awaiting their next turn of duty, moored on the buoys at Gravesend. They were included in the takeover by Howard Smith Towage Ltd in 1993, and in 1994 the pair transferred to Swansea where they took the local names **Langland** and **Caswell** respectively. Four years later they moved to Howard Smith (Humber) Ltd, Grimsby, and were renamed **Lady Joan** and **Lady Theresa**. In 2001 they were sold to Survey & Supply (Grimsby) and their names were shortened to **Joan** and **Theresa** respectively. The tugs are believed to have been sold to Hogg of Grimsby in 2004 and were still in existence in 2011.

(The late John Wiltshire)

In 2000 Dover Harbour Board sold its two Voith Schneider tractor tugs, the **Deft** and **Dextrous**. They passed to Howard Smith Towage Ltd as **Shorne** and **Cobham** for use on the Thames. They were built in 1984 by McTay Marine Ltd at Bromborough and were twin-unit tugs with a bollard pull of 29 tonnes. They passed to Adsteam (UK) Ltd in August 2001 and the **Shorne** is seen in Adsteam colours on 26 October 2003. In 2006 she was transferred to Humber Tugs Ltd, and renamed **HT Scimitar**. The Adsteam group passed to Svitzer Marine Ltd in 2007, and the **HT Scimitar** was later transferred to the south east Wales fleet based at Newport along with the **HT Cutlass** (formerly **Cobham**). In 2013 the **HT Scimitar** and **HT Cutlass** were shipped out to Venezuela to join the Svitzer (Americas) Ltd fleet.

(Dominic McCall)

The **Svitzer Anglia** was new to Alexandra Towing Co (London) Ltd as **Sun Anglia**. She was completed in 1985 by McTay Marine Ltd, Bromborough, as the final vessel in a series of three similar tugs and replaced the **Avenger** of 1962. The first was the Gravesend-based **Sun Thames** (page 66/67) followed in 1984 by the **Bramley Moore** which was based on the Mersey. The **Sun Anglia** was fitted for fire-fighting and was propelled by two Voith Schneider units. At 3492bhp she was a lot more powerful than **Sun Thames** and had a bollard pull of 38½ tonnes. She was eventually renamed **Adsteam Anglia** in early 2006 and was absorbed into Svitzer fleet from 2007, taking the name **Svitzer Anglia** in 2008. As such she is seen on 30 May 2009. In 2013 she joined the **HT Scimitar** and **HT Cutlass** when all three tugs were shipped out to Venezuela for further service with Svitzer (Americas) Ltd.

(Simon Smith)

Passing Gravesend on 18 May 2008 is Svitzer's twin-unit Voith Schneider tractor tug **Adsteam Mercia**. This tug was delivered new on 20 August 1990 as **Sun Mercia**. She was completed by McTay Marine Ltd at Bromborough for the Alexandra Towing Co Ltd, and was a larger and more powerful development of the **Sun Anglia**. The **Sun Mercia** was powered by a pair of Ruston 6RK270M diesels developing 3860bhp. This gave her a bollard pull of 43 tonnes and a speed of 12 knots. As can be seen by the platform connecting the tops of her funnels, she is equipped for fire-fighting. She remained based at Gravesend often being employed on coastal towing duties and passed to Howard Smith in 1993. Following the Adsteam takeover in 2001 the **Sun Mercia** was later renamed **Adsteam Mercia** in June 2005. She became part of the Svitzer Marine Ltd group from 2007 and renamed **Svitzer Mercia** in 2008. In 2016 she was helping out in the River Tyne-based fleet.

(Simon Smith)

As previously mentioned, Australian tug operator Howard Smith Towage took over all the UK operations of the Alexandra Towing Company in March 1993 and soon after the tugs began to receive the livery of their new owner. The **Sun Surrey** was the sistership of the **Sun Sussex** (next page) and both dated from 1992. The **Sun Surrey** is a fire-fighting tug with a speed of 12½ knots. This view of her dates from 3 October 1999. She passed from Howard Smith to Adsteam (UK) Ltd in 2001, and three years later was transferred to the Southampton fleet. The **Sun Surrey** was renamed **Adsteam Surrey** in 2005 before passing to the Svitzer Marine Ltd in 2007. In 2009 she was renamed **Svitzer Surrey**, and in 2016 was based at Belfast.

(Bernard McCall)

Arriving at Gravesend from Richards (Shipbuilders) Ltd, Great Yarmouth, in July 1992, the **Sun Sussex** was the last new tug delivered to Alexandra Towing Co Ltd. She was more or less identical to the **Sun Surrey** which had entered service the previous March. The **Sun Sussex** was a large twin-unit Voith Schneider tug of 378grt and with a fire-fighting capability. A bollard pull of 42 tonnes was achievable and power came from a pair of Ruston diesels with a combined output of 3826bhp. She was fairly new in this view from July 1992. The **Sun Sussex** was renamed **Adsteam Sussex** in 2005, passing to Svitzer Marine Ltd in 2007. At this point she became **Svitzer Sussex**. She later left the Thames and has worked at Southampton and Liverpool, but in 2016 was stationed at Belfast.

(Barry Crickmore)

In 2003 Adsteam Marine transferred two large harbour tugs from Australia to the Adsteam (UK) Ltd operation. These were the **Redcliffe** of 1986 and **Gurrong** of 2000. The **Gurrong** had been new to Howard Smith at Melbourne passing to Adsteam Marine in 2002. She had been launched at the Fremantle yard of Oceanfast Marine Pty Ltd and was completed in New Zealand by Northport Engineering Ltd, Whangarei. The **Gurrong** has a gross tonnage of 495 and her main engines comprise two 6-cyl Daihatsu diesels delivering 4894bhp. These drive a pair of Z-peller propulsion units that give the tug a bollard pull of 63 tonnes. Upon arrival in the UK the **Gurrong** was initially stationed at Gravesend and we see her off Northfleet Hope Container Terminal on 8 August 2004. In 2005 she was renamed **Adsteam Victory** and became part of the Medway-based fleet, passing into the Svitzer Marine Ltd fleet in 2007. She was renamed **Svitzer Victory** the same year, and in 2016 remains at work in the Thames estuary and the River Medway.

(Ian Willett)

Four new tugs were delivered to Svitzer Marine Ltd in 2003/04 from the Spanish shipyard Astilleros Zamakona, Viscaya. The **Svitzer Brunel** was the second tug and followed the **Svitzer Bristol** into service in the Avonmouth and Portbury-based fleet. The final pair emerged as **Svitzer Bootle** and **Svitzer Bidston** for the Mersey fleet. The **Svitzer Brunel** has a gross tonnage of 366 and is equipped for fire-fighting which includes a self-protection spray. She is a powerful tug of 4087bhp and her twin 6-cyl Niigata diesels give her a bollard pull of around 58½ tonnes. Propulsion is by way of two Niigata ZP-31 azimuthing units. By the time of this image on 30 September 2014, the **Svitzer Brunel** had been transferred to the Gravesend fleet where she remained in 2016. Her sister **Svitzer Bristol** was working on the Humber in 2016.

(Ian Willett)

BP Shipping decided to establish its own tug fleet to serve the Coryton oil terminal located in the Thames estuary, and in 2003 ordered three powerful vessels from Damen Shipyards in the Netherlands. They had to fulfil four roles, fire-fighting, towing, escorting and pollution control. Damen's well proven ASD3211 design was chosen, which since its introduction in the mid-1990s had been much improved, and now offered a much higher bollard pull. The three tugs were delivered in 2005 as **Castle Point**, **Corringham** and **Stanford**. Registered in the Isle of Man, they were owned by BP Shipping Ltd and managed by Targe Towing Ltd of Montrose. Targe already had experience managing tugs for BP at Hound Point on the Firth of Forth. The **Castle Point** is noted here at Coryton terminal 2 on 30 May 2009. Following closure of Coryton terminal in 2012 the **Castle Point** and **Stanford** were sold to Svitzer Ltd. The **Castle Point** was renamed **Svitzer Castle**, and in 2017 she was active in Svitzer's Humber fleet.

(Simon Smith)

Another of the trio is the **Corringham** which is noted on station at Coryton on 22 May 2010. These tugs had a gross tonnage of 385 and an overall length of just under 106 feet. Their hulls were constructed in Poland by Stocznia Remontowa Nauta SA, Gdynia, and the tugs were completed in the Netherlands by Scheepswerf Damen BV, Gorinchem. They are powered by a pair of 6-cyl MaK 6M25 diesels which together develop 5310bhp at 750rpm. This output drives a pair of Rolls-Royce Aquamaster US255CP propulsion units which incorporate controllable-pitch propellers. The recorded bollard pull ahead is 66.7 tonnes while that astern is 62.6 tonnes. The tug's fire-fighting and self-protection dousing system is supplied by a pair of Nijhuis fire pumps, and the two remotely-controlled water/foam monitors are located on a platform between the funnels. With the closure of the Coryton terminal in 2012, the **Corringham** did not pass to Svitzer, but was retained by BP Shipping Ltd and transferred to Hound Point on the Firth of Forth, where she became part of the BP tug fleet.

(Simon Smith)

Adsteam Marine took delivery of a pair of Damen ASD Tug 2411 units in February 2006. They were built in Vietnam by Song Cam Shipyard of Hai Phong, and transported by ship to Rotterdam. Here they were completed by Scheepswerf Damen BV, Gorinchem, as **Adsteam Harty** and **Adsteam Warden** and delivered for service at Sheerness. They were intended to tow over the bow using a hydraulically-driven split-drum winch. Consequently the aft deck features only a centrally-located towing post. These powerful fire-fighting tugs have a bollard pull of 68 tonnes and have two 16-cyl Caterpillar diesels which drive a pair of Rolls-Royce US255 propulsion units. By the summer of 2007 both tugs formed part of the Svitzer Marine fleet, and were renamed **Svitzer Harty** and **Svitzer Warden** respectively. The latter is noted at the new deep-sea container port at London Gateway, on 17 May 2014.

(Simon Smith)

Dutch tug operator KOTUG moved into the UK market in 2013 establishing KOTUG (UK) Ltd. With an office at London Gateway, they planned to compete for a slice of the new container port's towage business. Tugs are usually based at Thameshaven and London Gateway. Normally based at Rotterdam the *SD Seal* worked on the Thames in 2013 and again during the summer of 2016. She is seen here off Erith on 3 August 2016. The *SD Seal* was one of a class of four similar tugs purchased by KOTUG to the Ramparts 3200 design, and was built in Turkey in 2008 by Med Yilmaz Tersanesi AS at Zonguldak. Delivered as the *Medyilmaz 06* to Med Marine Towage, Istanbul, she was immediately resold to Elisabeth Ltd under the Maltese flag and renamed *SD Seal*. She was managed by KOTUG International BV. She is a Z-drive tug with a bollard pull of 65 tonnes ahead and 60 tonnes astern. In May 2016 KOTUG had four tugs based on the Thames estuary.

(Simon Smith)

The rotor tug first appeared in 1999 with the entry into service at Rotterdam and Bremerhaven of four vessels for KOTUG. The concept was originally patented by KOTUG president Ton Kooren and provides a unique propulsion system with three fully azimuthing Schottel units. Two are mounted forward and the third is aft of the centreline and replaces the traditional skeg. Two later examples were based at the London Gateway terminal for KOTUG from 2013. These were the *RT Champion* and *RT Leader* which dated from 2011, and are RT80-32 type Rotor tugs constructed in Japan by Niigata Shipbuilding & Repair Inc. The *RT Champion* is noted near Northfleet on 16 February 2014. She features three Niigata Z-Peller FFP ZP-31 propulsion units that give her an ahead bollard pull of 84 tonnes. By 2016 both the *RT Champion* and the *RT Leader* had been redeployed, and were working for KOTUG in the Brunei region of Malaysia.

(Laurie Rufus)

The **Svitzer London** was delivered to the Gravesend-based fleet of Svitzer Marine Ltd in May 2014. She is a standard Damen ASD Tug 3212 and was completed in Vietnam by Song Cam Damen Shipyards Ltd at Hai Phong, and completed by Damen Shiprepair Rotterdam BV, Rotterdam. She is a powerful tug with a bollard pull of 82 tonnes towing ahead. The **Svitzer** is powered by two 16-cyl Caterpillar diesels which drive a pair of Rolls Royce US255 azimuthing propulsion units. She was designed to do most of her ship handling over the bow, and her sole towing winch is mounted on her foredeck. To tow from her aft deck, a quick-release hook and towing bits are provided. This view of the **Svitzer London** was taken on 9 June 2016 as the tug was returning from Grays to her moorings at Gravesend. The substantial fendering fore and aft is a noteworthy feature.

(Ian Willett)

The **SD Shark** was another example of the class of four Ramparts 3200 design tugs purchased by KOTUG. She was also built in Turkey in 2008 by Med Yilmaz Tersanesi AS at Zonguldak and launched as the **Medyilmaz 04**. Initially delivered to Med Marine Towage Ltd, Istanbul, she passed to SD Shark Ltd, Valletta (KOTUG International) in June 2008 as **SD Shark**. She has a gross tonnage of 486 and is powered by a pair of 16-cyl Caterpillar diesels developing 5218bhp and driving a pair of Schottel SRP1515 propulsion units. She is equipped for fire-fighting and has towing winches located both forward and aft. On 7 April 2016 Royal Boskalis Westminster N.V. and KOTUG International B.V. merged their European operations to form KOTUG Smit Towage. The new operation included 65 tugs based at 11 ports. The **SD Shark** is seen passing Gravesend on 8 October 2016 and wearing the new KOTUG Smit Towage colours.

(Stuart Emery)

The ***Portwey*** is one of a small number of steam tugs in the UK that have been privately preserved and restored to full working order. The ***Portwey*** is noted at the Queen's Diamond Jubilee Pageant on 3 June 2012. She is moored just upstream from Tower Bridge and is remarkably bathed in sunlight, on what was generally a very dark and wet day. This twin-screw tug was launched in August 1927 at Govan on the Clyde by Harland & Wolff Ltd and delivered the following April to Portland & Weymouth Coaling Co Ltd, Portland, and registered in Weymouth. She was coal-fired and her machinery consists of a pair of compound steam engines of 330ihp. She worked at Dartmouth from 1938 and was with the Falmouth Docks & Engineering Co Ltd, Falmouth, from 1951 until her sale for preservation in 1967. In 1982 the ***Portwey*** was donated to the Maritime Trust, London, and in 2000 was in the care of the Steam Tug PORTWEY Trust, and usually kept at the West India Dock, London. She has been the subject of a great deal of restoration over the years and is regularly in steam.

(Stuart Emery)